The Updated Pocket Guide to Discover the Hidden Treasures of Languedoc and Roussillon Culture, Must-See Attraction Sites & Useful Tips for Family, Solo Travellers, Seniors and First-Timers

Languedoc and Roussillon Travel Guide 2024

ROLAND RICHARD

Copyright 2023. Roland Richard.

All rights Reserved!

No part of this book may be reproduced, stored in a retrieval system, or transmitted in any form or by any means, electronic, mechanical, photocopying, recording, or otherwise, without the prior written permission of the copyright owner.

Table of Contents

Table of Contents	3
Languedoc and Roussillon Region	6
Introduction	7
Welcome to Languedoc and Roussillon!	11
What's New?: Languedoc and Roussillon in 2024	11
How to Use This Guide	12
Chapter 1	15
Getting Started	15
Organising Your Travel	15
The Ideal Time to Visit	17
Essential Travel Items	18
Local Customs and Traditions	19
Chapter 2	21
The Regions of Languedoc and Roussillon	21
Description of the Regions	21
Languedoc	22
Roussillon	22
Climate and Geography	23
Background History	24
Chapter 3	27
Hidden Treasures of Languedoc and Roussillon	27
Gorgeous Towns and Villages	27
Distinct Cultural Encounters	32
Savoury Treats	36
Local Craft and Art Trade	38

Chapter 4	42
Must-See Attractions	42
Famous Historical Sites	42
Wonders of Nature	45
Museums and Galleries	47
Outside Activities	50
Chapter 5	53
Exploring the Local Culture	53
Festivals & Celebrations	53
Local Crafts	56
Food and Drink	58
Dancing and Music	60
Chapter 6	62
Insider Tips for Different Types of Travelers	62
Enchanting Wineries For Families	63
Solo Traveler's Guide	64
Advice For Senior Travelers	66
First-Timers' Checklist	68
Chapter 7	71
Accommodation and Dining	71
Options for Lodging	71
Eateries and Coffee Shops	73
Specialties of Local Cuisine	75
Chapter 8	78
Transportation and Getting Around	78
Travelling to Roussillon and Languedoc	78
Local Transportation in the Regions	79
Cycling	81

Boat Tours	81
Car Rental Tips	81
Chapter 9	**84**
Safety and Health	**84**
Safety Considerations	84
Emergency Phone Numbers	86
Medical and Health Facilities	86
Chapter 10	**90**
Language and Communication	**90**
Basics of Language	90
Handy Expressions	91
Tips On Communication	92
Chapter 11	**95**
Practical Information	**95**
Currency and Banking	95
Local Rules and Statutes	96
Cultural Awareness	97
Traffic Rules	97
Chapter 12	**98**
Itineraries and Day Trips	**98**
One-Week Itinerary for Roussillon and Languedoc	98
Two-Week Exploration Itinerary	99
Recommended Day Trips	100
Conclusion	**103**
Share Your Feedback	104

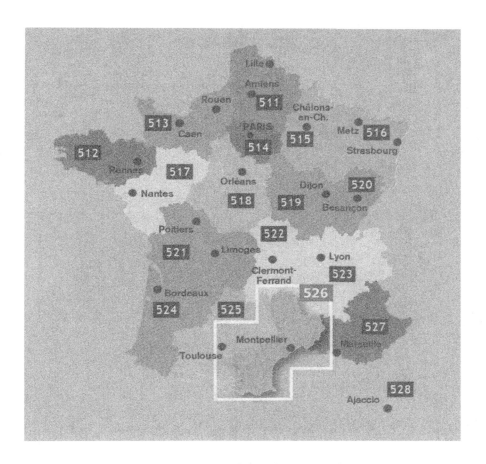

Languedoc and Roussillon Region

Introduction

My trip through this region of southern France was an unforgettable experience that will always have a particular place in my heart. I was captivated by the ageless charm and rich legacy of this remarkable region, with its undulating vineyards and historic stone villages.

I started my tour in the mediaeval walled town of Carcassonne, which felt like a doorway to another period.

It felt like I had slipped into the pages of a live fairy tale as I wandered through its maze-like alleyways, marvelled at its towering walls, and walked down its cobblestone streets.

I was in awe of Carcassonne's 12th-century architecture, vibrant market squares, and well-preserved history, which provided a stark reminder of the past's continuing influence. Food and wine lovers are sure to find refuge in Languedoc and Roussillon. I remember quite well spending an evening in Montpellier, eating outside at a small café. A lavish display of flavorful fish, strong olives, aromatic herbs, and a glass of locally made wine decorated the table. I was taken to the very centre of the region's culinary culture with every dish and drink—a gastronomic adventure I won't soon forget.

Wandering off the well-travelled routes, I discovered charming towns like Collioure, a jewel of the coast with pastel-coloured buildings, and Minerve, high above a shimmering river. These undiscovered treasures provided a genuine window into the history and way of life of the area, resembling postcards come to life.

While a last-minute trip to a bustling village festival in Limoux had me dancing to the sounds of traditional music as the sun set, Perpignan's art galleries and craft workshops honoured the region's creative spirit. Nature lovers will find heaven in Languedoc and Roussillon. I went on hikes in the breathtaking Gorges du Tarn, where a glistening river serenaded my path and soaring limestone cliffs hugged me. I was mesmerised by the sight of flamingos in the Étang de Bages-Sigean lagoons and the dreamy surroundings of the Cathar castles, which served as a constant reminder of the infinite beauty of the planet.

The real friendliness and warmth of the locals were two of the things I treasured most about my trip. I met a winemaker by coincidence in a tiny village, and we had a wonderful talk. He extended a kind invitation for me to visit his family's property. There, over a bottle of their best vintage, I shared stories and learned about the nuances of winemaking. These interpersonal relationships were what made my visit a genuine and rewarding experience.

More than just vacation spots, Languedoc and Roussillon are dynamic mosaics of culture, history, and breathtaking scenery. I left this enthralling area with a stronger appreciation for life's small joys, a deep love for French culture, and an unquenchable desire to come back and discover even more of this undiscovered treasure.

I strongly recommend this trip to all daring travellers since there is a tale ready to be told by each person who sets foot in this captivating country.

Welcome to Languedoc and Roussillon!

Welcome to the mesmerising regions of Languedoc and Roussillon, where rich cultural traditions, stunning scenery, and a long history combine to make for an incredible vacation. Tucked away in the heart of southern France, these areas are teeming with undiscovered gems just waiting to be unearthed.

Languedoc and Roussillon provide a complex tapestry of experiences that appeal to all kinds of travellers, from the sun-drenched vineyards to the ancient cobblestone towns.

What's New?: Languedoc and Roussillon in 2024

I am excited to share with you the most recent information and insider recommendations for an even more amazing trip in the Languedoc and Roussillon Travel Guide 2024. Take in the culinary creations of up-and-coming local chefs, tour recently discovered ancient sites, and take part in distinctive cultural celebrations that have developed over generations. I've searched the area to find the newest and most fascinating things Languedoc and Roussillon have to offer.

How to Use This Guide

This guide is intended to serve as your travel guide for an amazing experience. Suggestions inside are customised to meet your needs, whether you're a family looking for special moments, a lone traveller hunting for hidden treasures, an elderly person looking for a relaxing getaway, or a first-time visitor ready to explore.

★ *Get Around with Ease*: You can easily discover the information you need thanks to the comprehensive table of contents and user-friendly structure of this guide.

★ *Local Insights:* You are provided historical anecdotes, practical tips, and local insights throughout the guide to help you get to know the real Languedoc and Roussillon.

★ *Custom Itineraries:* Find carefully designed itineraries to make sure you don't miss the must-see places, whether you have a week or a month to visit.

★ *Cultural Immersion:* Take in everything that the lively local culture has to offer, from wine tastings to artisan workshops and eye-catching festivals.

★ *Safety and Useful Advice:* Learn about health and safety issues, as well as useful advice on bargaining, communicating, and local legislation.

A journey through this fascinating region awaits you; it is filled with opportunities to find hidden gems, sample delicious food, and create lifelong memories. In 2024, you have the opportunity to explore Languedoc and

Roussillon, and this guide will help you discover their allure.

Bronze Face Fountain

Chapter 1

Getting Started

Organising Your Travel

Do you have a plan for your visit to the Languedoc and Roussillon regions? Plan your journey to Languedoc and Roussillon with these useful suggestions in mind:

1. *Outline your passions:* To develop a well-organized itinerary, decide what you want to see and do, such as historical landmarks, local culture, or outdoor activities.
2. *Uncover Diverse Regions:* Roussillon and Languedoc have a range of places to visit. Look into and select locations that suit your preferences, be they beach towns, vineyards, or quaint villages.
3. *Reservations for lodging:* Book well in advance, particularly during the busiest travel times. Choose an accommodation that fits your needs and budget—there are everything from five-star hotels to more affordable options.
4. *Plan your transportation:* Choose your means of transportation to get around the area. Renting a car offers freedom, but public transport is a convenient way to get from one city to another. Choose the one that most closely fits your itinerary for travel.

The Ideal Time to Visit

Consider the following variations in the seasons while making travel plans:

- *Spring and Autumn:* These months, which run from April to June and September to November, are great for sightseeing and outdoor activities because of the nice weather and lack of crowds.
- *Summer:* Come in July and August if you like bright events and warm weather. Remember that this is the busiest travel season, so higher rates and more people are to be expected.
- *Winter:* While December through February is calmer and more laid back, some attractions could only be open for a limited time at this time. If you want more privacy, this is the best time to go.

Essential Travel Items

The following items are necessary to pack and get ready for your trip:

1. *Appropriate Dress:* Dress appropriately for the weather and the activities you have scheduled. Essentials include light summer attire, layers for cooler temperatures, and comfortable walking shoes.
2. *Travel Documents:* Make sure you have your visas, passports, and travel insurance. For safety, keep both digital and physical copies. It is essential to keep a copy on you while moving around the region
3. *Finance and Payment:* Keep credit cards and cash on you. Even though credit cards are accepted almost everywhere, it's a good idea to carry extra cash, particularly in smaller towns.

4. *Basic French Phrases:* Being able to communicate with locals in French will greatly improve your vacation experience.

Local Customs and Traditions

Remember the following local traditions to guarantee a happy, calm, and pleasurable visit:

1. *Greetings and Courtesies:* When entering stores and restaurants, it is traditional to say polite greetings such as "Bonjour" (good morning) and "Bonsoir" (good evening). Greetings are generally exchanged through handshakes. Remember that you want to be seen as friendly.

2. *Dining Etiquette:* Savour your meals and embrace the French dining culture. Since supper and lunch are informal events, give yourself plenty of time to savour

your cuisine and the companionship of your other diners.

3. *Cultural Respect:* Wear modest clothing when you visit houses of worship or other local residences. Before taking pictures of people or their property, you should always get their permission.
4. *Tipping:* Although not required, it's common to offer a little tip for exceptional service or to round up the total.

Your trip to Languedoc and Roussillon will be more pleasurable and respectful to the local way of life if you comprehend and put these suggestions into practice. You will find all the information you need in this guide.

Keep reading!

Chapter 2

The Regions of Languedoc and Roussillon

Description of the Regions

The southern regions of France, Languedoc and Roussillon, are like two different characters in a compelling play. Although each has its personality, when combined, they tell a captivating story that takes place in the beautiful setting of the Mediterranean.

Languedoc

The more expansive and diversified of the two regions, Languedoc is renowned for its distinctive landscape. There are vast grasslands, meandering vineyards, and a stunning Mediterranean coastline with exquisite beaches. This area is renowned for its superb wines, produced in the numerous vineyards that dot the landscape, ranging from bold reds to delicate whites.

The dynamic cities of Languedoc, such as Toulouse and Montpellier, are teeming with old-world charm, modern vitality, and cultural diversity. The magnificent mediaeval city of Carcassonne, a UNESCO World Heritage Site, is a highlight.

Roussillon

The smaller and more southern region of Roussillon, on the other hand, has a certain allure due to its

Mediterranean coastline, rugged topography, and distinctive French and Catalan cultural fusion.

West of Roussillon, the Pyrenees Mountains offer a striking landscape, while the Mediterranean's Vermilion Coast dazzles with its clear-blue waves and deep-red cliffs. The language, customs, and food of this area are all strongly influenced by Catalan culture. You will be engrossed in a fascinating fusion of Spanish and French culture.

Climate and Geography

Gaining an understanding of the topography and climate of these areas will enable you to get the most out of your trip:

- **Geography:** The varied terrain of Languedoc includes wide-open vineyards, quaint undulating hills, and the appeal of the Mediterranean shore. In the meantime, the rich topography of Roussillon includes craggy mountains, quaint seaside villages, and the vibrant colours of the Vermilion Coast, which serve as an artistic inspiration.

- **Climate:** The Mediterranean climate is shared by Roussillon and Languedoc. Beachgoers and outdoor enthusiasts can enjoy plenty of sunshine during the hot and dry summers. With fewer visitors, the mild and rainy winters give a certain type of appeal. Travellers can be certain of year-round appeal due to this climate, as each season has its distinct charm.

Background History

These areas are treasure troves of historical information and cultural diversity, not just gorgeous scenery.

- **Cathar Legacy:** The flourishing Catholic religious movement in the 12th and 13th centuries left an indelible effect on Languedoc's history. The Cathar legacy has a connection with the history of the area, leading to the creation of remarkable castles and strongholds. The most famous of these, and proof of Languedoc's historical importance, is the mediaeval fortress of Carcassonne.

- **Roman Legacy:** The well-preserved Roman sites in Languedoc and Roussillon demonstrate the Roman Empire's lasting legacy. A view into the magnificence of the Roman era is provided by the aqueduct Pont du Gard, the Roman theatre at Nîmes, and numerous archaeological finds.

- **Catalan Ancestry:** Because of its closeness to Spain, Roussillon has a rich history influenced by its Catalan ancestry. This impact can be seen in the food, festivals, and the fact that some locals speak Catalan.

You will become enmeshed in Languedoc and Roussillon's history as you travel through their towns, villages, and historic sites. Every location and landmark narrates a tale, providing a greater understanding of the distinct personality and diverse cultural fabric of the area.

Chapter 3

Hidden Treasures of Languedoc and Roussillon

Gorgeous Towns and Villages

Enchanting towns and villages surround Languedoc and Roussillon, luring visitors with their timeless elegance and genuine charm. Discover these undiscovered treasures that encapsulate the spirit of southern France:

★ **Minerve**

Address: 34210 Aude, France; Minerve

Notable Landmark: **Pont Naturel**, a naturally occurring stone bridge with breathtaking views of the canyon and its surroundings.

With stone homes and cobblestone walkways, Minerve is a mediaeval marvel perched high above a river. It's a historic bridge and pleasant squares take you back in time.

 ★ **Collioure**

Address: Collioure, 66190 Pyrénées-Orientales, France

Special Landmark: **Château Royal de Collioure** - Discover this storied castle with sweeping views of the coastline and the Mediterranean.

Languedoc and Roussillon Travel Guide 2024

Collioure, a picturesque fishing community with pastel-coloured homes, a mediaeval castle, and lively art galleries, is tucked away on the Vermilion Coast. This allure is enhanced by the Mediterranean setting.

★ **Cucugnan**

Address: Cucugnan, 11350 Aude, France

Notable Landmark: A unique landmark is the mediaeval castle **Château de Quéribus**, which is built atop a rocky ridge and provides breathtaking views of the Mediterranean and the Pyrenees.

The mediaeval castle towers over this charming village, which is encircled by olive and wine groves. Its winding lanes are perfect for strolls, and the vistas of the surrounding countryside are stunning.

★ Eus

Address: Eus, 66500 Pyrénées-Orientales, France

Notable Landmark: **Eglise Saint-Vincent**, a quaint church with flower-covered facades and cobblestone streets near the centre of the village.

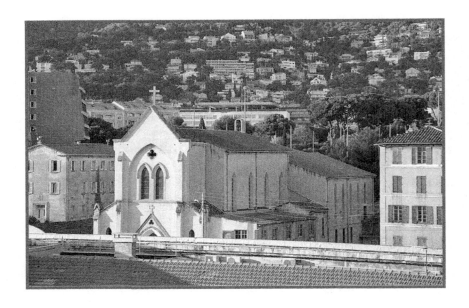

Eus, one of "Les Plus Beaux Villages de France" (The Most Beautiful Villages of France), is renowned for its picturesque mediaeval atmosphere, flower-covered façade, and meandering, narrow alleyways.

Distinct Cultural Encounters

Take advantage of these exceptional opportunities to fully immerse yourself in the lively local cultures of Languedoc and Roussillon:

★ **Cathar Nation Exploration**

Unique Point of Interest: **The City of Carcassonne** - Discover the unique towers and fortifications of this mediaeval castle, which is recognised as a UNESCO World Heritage Site.

Discover the mediaeval past of the Cathar region by touring the historic village of Lastours, the fortress of Carcassonne, and the Cathar castles located on the mountains.

★ **Traditional Celebrations: The Limoux Carnival**

Fascinating Information: Take part in the bright parades, colourful costumes and traditional music at Limoux's colourful funfair.

Attend one of the region's traditional festivals to feel the vibrant energy there. Not to be missed are the **Feria de Nîmes,** a celebration of bullfighting and music, and the **Limoux Carnival,** which is known for its vibrant parades.

★ **Wine Tasting at Château L'Hospitalet in the Vineyards**

Interesting Data: This winery, tucked away among vineyards, offers tastings and guided tours that give visitors an inside look at the winemaking process. Take a tour across the expansive Languedoc vineyards and sample a variety of top-notch wines. A lot of vineyards provide guided tours that give visitors an understanding of the winemaking process.

★ **Sail in the Canal du Midi**

Departure Point: Port Lauragais, 31290 Avignonet-Lauragais, France

Interesting Data: Take a leisurely boat ride through quaint villages and scenic landscapes along the historic Canal du Midi.

Enjoy a leisurely boat ride along the UNESCO-designated World Heritage Site, the ancient Canal du Midi. Take in the breathtaking scenery, charming towns, and engineering feats of this 17th-century canal.

Medieval Carcassonne, France

Savoury Treats

Culinary paradise Languedoc and Roussillon offer a delicious combination of flavours that will entice your palate:

★ **Castelnaudary's Cassoulet Restaurant: La Belle Époque**

Exciting Information: Visit this well-known restaurant in the centre of Castelnaudary to savour a real cassoulet.

Savour the famous Castelnaudary cassoulet, a filling stew of white beans, beef, and sausages. This dish is a speciality from the area that showcases its culinary skills.

★ **Seafood in Collioure**

Restaurant: Le Neptune

Exciting Information: This quaint eatery offers fresh seafood while providing a glimpse of Collioure's harbour.

In Collioure, where the catch of the day is turned into culinary masterpieces, savour fresh seafood. Restaurants beside the water provide the ideal atmosphere for savouring the bounty of the Mediterranean.

★ **Saturday Market Picnic**

Enjoy a picnic at the Pezenas Market

Interesting Data: Grab some fresh produce from the market and enjoy a picnic in one of Pezenas' old squares.

Travel to Pezenas, a town famous for its vibrant market. Enjoy a picnic in the town's charming squares with artisanal bread, cured meats, and cheeses that are locally produced.

20 mins

★ Uzès's Local Markets

Exciting Information: Treat your senses to a sensory feast by perusing the lively Uzès market, which is well-known for its truffles, cheeses, and olives.

Discover the lively markets of Uzès and indulge in local specialities such as cheeses, olives, and truffles. Interact with regional suppliers to get a genuine eating experience.

Local Craft and Art Trade

Learn about the rich traditions and talented craftspeople of Languedoc and Roussillon to uncover their artistic souls:

[handwritten note: 20 mins / Nana?]

★ Pottery in Saint-Quentin-la-Poterie

Pottery Studio: Terre Figuière

Interesting Data: Come to this pottery workshop to see the artists at work crafting one-of-a-kind ceramics and maybe even bring home a handmade memento.

This hamlet is well known for its ceramics studios. Visit the workshops where skilled potters create one-of-a-kind ceramic items ranging from decorative to useful kitchenware.

★ Perpignan's Catalan Art Scene

Art Center: Hyacinthe Rigaud Art Center

Interesting Data: Come to the Perpignan Contemporary Art Centre to immerse yourself in the dynamic Catalan art scene.

With its strong Catalan influence, Perpignan is a centre for modern art. Explore galleries such as the Hyacinthe Rigaud Art Centre to get a taste of the colourful Catalan art scene.

★ **Blanquette Tapestry in Blanquette**

Workshop: Atelier La Vie en Laine

Interesting Data: Come discover the craft of creating classic tapestries in Blanquette at this quaint studio.

Blanquette's ancient tapestry craft is well-known. See firsthand how these exquisite woven artworks are made by visiting nearby workshops.

★ **The Beziers Flea Markets**

Exciting Information: Visit the vibrant flea markets in Beziers to look for unique handicrafts and hidden gems.

Beziers has vibrant flea markets with vintage handicrafts, vintage apparel, and antique furniture. Talk to local sellers to find hidden gems and show your support for regional craftspeople.

Take a trip that goes beyond tourism to discover the true essence of Languedoc and Roussillon, which includes its quaint villages, rich cultural traditions, delectable cuisine, and handcrafted goods.

Chapter 4

Must-See Attractions

Famous Historical Sites

The stories of triumph, mystery, and cultural richness abound on the pages of Languedoc and Roussillon, which are like living historical novels. Discover these historical sites that will take you back hundreds of years:

★ La Cité de Carcassonne

Address: 1 Rue Viollet-le-Duc, 11000 Carcassonne, France

Exciting Information: Explore the flawlessly preserved mediaeval stronghold of La Cité de Carcassonne, a world straight out of a fairy tale. Admire its double ring of towers, drawbridges, and defensive walls. Don't miss the stunning stained glass windows at the Basilica of Saint-Nazaire.

★ Pont du Gard

Address: 400 Route du Pont du Gard, 30210 Vers-Pont-du-Gard, France

Interesting Fact: The Pont du Gard, an old Roman aqueduct, is a reminder of the Roman Empire's mastery of engineering. Not only is this three-tiered bridge a marvel, but it also provides a picturesque backdrop for strolls and picnics.

★ Château de Quéribus   3 hrs

Address: 11350 Cucugnan, France

Exciting Information: One of the "Five Sons of Carcassonne," Château de Quéribus is situated atop a rocky peak and is a part of the Cathar Castle network. Its advantageous location affords truly stunning panoramic vistas.

49 min

★ Roman Theater of Nîmes

Address: Boulevard des Arènes, 30000 Nîmes, France

Interesting Data: Take in the magnificence of the Nîmes Roman Theatre. Imagine the thunderous applause from the crowd when gladiators used to fight in this pristine arena. The theatre is transformed into a platform for world-class performances during the annual Nîmes Festival.

Wonders of Nature

Languedoc and Roussillon are places where nature displays her beauty in a multitude of ways, beckoning you to discover captivating landscapes and breathtaking marvels:

★ **Gorges du Tarn**

Address: Gorges du Tarn, France

Exciting Information: Carve your way through the canyons du Tarn's limestone canyons. Adventurers can explore this natural treasure by hiking along the cliff edges, kayaking on the meandering river, or just taking in the breath-blowing views.

★ **Étang de Bages-Sigean**

Address: D6009, 11130 Sigean, France

Interesting Information: Étang de Bages-Sigean is a coastal lagoon that is home to a wide variety of bird species, making it a haven for birdwatchers. The striking pink tones of flamingos set against the serene waters make for an enchanting sight.

★ **Castles Cathar**

Interesting Information: Discover the mysteries of the rocky promontories that house the Cathar Castles. Two intriguing episodes in the history of the area are Puilaurens, tucked away in the Pyrenean foothills, and Montségur, regarded as the final stronghold of the Cathars.

★ Cévennes National Park

Address: Cévennes National Park, France

Interesting Fact: Those who enjoy the outdoors will find paradise in Cévennes National Park. Hike along paths through thick forests, discover tumbling waterfalls, and take in the clean mountain air. Look out for the variety of species that inhabit this park.

Museums and Galleries

Discover the creative and historical legacy of Languedoc and Roussillon by visiting museums and galleries that highlight the areas' cultural tapestry:

★ Musée Fabre

Address: 39 Boulevard Bonne Nouvelle, 34000 Montpellier, France

Exciting Information: The Musée Fabre in Montpellier offers a voyage through art history rather than just a museum. With artwork ranging from Renaissance to modern pieces, the museum provides a thorough understanding of the development of art.

★ **Musée d'Art Moderne de Céret**

Address: 8 Boulevard Maréchal Joffre, 66400 Céret, France

The "Museum of Modern Art City," Céret, is home to a collection of works by prominent Fauvist artists like as Picasso and Braque. The town's important significance in the contemporary art movement is demonstrated by the collection housed in the museum.

★ Le Musée de l'Éphèbe

Address: Avenue des Campings, 34300 Le Cap d'Agde, France

Exciting Information: A maritime treasure trove can be found at the Musée de l'Éphèbe in Cap d'Agde. Explore the realm of underwater archaeology by examining items retrieved from historic shipwrecks, which feature the renowned bronze statue of Éphèbe.

★ Centre Pompidou-Metz

Address: 1 Parvis des Droits de l'Homme, 57020 Metz, France

Exciting Information: The Centre Pompidou-Metz is a singular cultural destination, even if it's not in Languedoc or Roussillon. The shows present modern art in an inventive and provocative way, and the building itself is a work of art.

Outside Activities

Experience the wild side of Languedoc and Roussillon, where a wide range of exhilarating activities are waiting for adventurers:

Hiking in the Pyrenees

Exciting Information: Discover the Pyrenees on foot via a network of routes by donning hiking boots. The Pyrenees provide treks for all skill levels, from easy family hikes on moderate slopes to strenuous climbs that yield breathtaking views.

Canoeing On The Orb River

Location: Roquebrun, France

Interesting Information: Canoe the Orb River and cross the picturesque Saint-Chinian wine district. This is a relaxing but worthwhile water experience because of the calm currents and lovely surroundings.

Cycling Along the Canal du Midi

Route: Canal du Midi Towpath

Pedal down the historic Canal du Midi, a UNESCO World Heritage Site. This is exciting information. The level towpath provides a picturesque route past quaint towns, old locks, and avenues of plane trees that provide shade.

Windsurfing in Leucate

Location: Leucate, France

Exciting Information: Leucate's high winds and perfect conditions make it a windsurfing haven that draws enthusiasts. The Mediterranean waters appeal for an adrenaline encounter regardless of your level of surfing expertise.

In Languedoc and Roussillon, every landmark, wonder, museum, and outdoor activity opens a new chapter in the fascinating tale of these remarkable regions. Set off on a voyage through time, nature, art, and adventure.

Chapter 5

Exploring the Local Culture

Festivals & Celebrations

The vibrant cultural scenes of Roussillon and Languedoc are emphasised by festivals and celebrations that erupt with enthusiasm. Put these exciting events on your calendar:

Carnival in Limoux

Location: Limoux, France

Interesting Information: The town is transformed into a riot of colour and happiness during the January–March Limoux Carnival. There are street parades, exciting music and a unique funfair experience with the quirky 'Blanquette' fight.

Feria de Nîmes

Location: Nîmes, France

Interesting Information: The Feria de Nîmes is a mesmerising celebration of street parties, music, and bullfighting that takes place in late May. Take in the festive mood as the city is transformed into a venue for dances and cultural events.

Fête de la Musique

Location: All around the country, including Roussillon and Languedoc

Exciting Information: On June 21, enjoy the Fête de la Musique, a day when squares and streets are filled with music. Savour musical offerings spanning from classical to modern, fostering a melodious festivity throughout the nation.

Festival of Sete Water Jousting

Location: Sète, France

Interesting Fact: Experience the Water Jousting Festival in July, an annual event that dates back to the 17th century. Boat teams compete in exciting jousting matches in front of boisterous spectators and lively music.

Local Crafts

Discover the artistic legacy of Languedoc and Roussillon by investigating regional handicrafts and workshops that highlight the inventiveness of the areas:

Pottery in Saint-Quentin-la-Poterie

Location: Saint-Quentin-la-Poterie, France

Interesting Information: Explore ceramic workshops like Terre Figuière by visiting the quaint village all year round. Interact with craftspeople, observe the creation of pottery, and possibly acquire a one-of-a-kind ceramic work of art.

Catalan Art in Perpignan

Location: Perpignan, France

Exciting Information: The year-round art scene in Perpignan is developing. Experience the strong artistic expression of Catalonia by visiting the Hyacinthe Rigaud Art Centre and other galleries, which host shows including both local and international talents.

Blanquette Tapestry in Blanquette

Location: Blanquette, France

Exciting Information: Learn the craft of creating tapestries at Blanquette's Atelier La Vie en Laine. Make plans to visit at any time of year to see the elaborate process used to create these stunning woven artworks.

The Beziers Flea Markets

Location: Beziers, France

Interesting Fact: Beziers has vibrant flea markets all year long. Discover hidden gems by interacting with local merchants, exploring the vibrant ambience, and searching for one-of-a-kind items.

Food and Drink

Enjoy the flavours of Languedoc and Roussillon by savouring the delicious food and well-known wines of the regions:

Cassoulet in Castelnaudary

Restaurant: La Belle Époque, Castelnaudary

Interesting Fact: La Belle Époque serves a hearty dish of cassoulet year-round, and Castelnaudary is the capital of this dish. Consider visiting in August for the Cassoulet Festival for a truly immersive culinary experience.

Seafood in Collioure

Restaurant: Le Neptune, Collioure

Exciting Information: You can have Collioure's seafood specialities all year round. Savour freshly caught seafood at Le Neptune while taking in views of the charming harbour and the Mediterranean beyond.

Picnicking in Pezenas

Market: Pezenas Saturday Market

Interesting Information: Every week, the Pezenas market is a treat. To assemble handmade bread, cured meats, and cheeses from the area for a pleasant picnic in the old squares, schedule your visit for a Saturday.

Uzès's Local Markets

Interesting Information: Every Wednesday and Saturday, Uzès has lively markets. Make plans to enjoy local specialities, interact with merchants, and take in the vibrant atmosphere.

Dancing and Music

Discover the rhythms of Roussillon and Languedoc through their traditional dances and music:

Flamenco in Perpignan

Exciting Information: Throughout the year, visit cosy flamenco bars in Perpignan. The intense performances highlight this historic dance and music form's creativity.

Jazz in Montpellier

Venue: Many Montpellier Jazz Clubs

Interesting Fact: The jazz culture in Montpellier is thriving all year round. For a captivating experience, visit ambient jazz clubs like Jam, where talented local and international musicians create a magical environment.

Traditional Folk Music in Céret

Event: Céret Cherry Festival (May)

Interesting Information: One of May's top events is the Céret Cherry Festival, which honours traditional folk music in addition to cherries. Participate in the celebrations, where upbeat music and dancing foster a happy vibe.

Sardana Dancing in Collioure

Location: Collioure, France

Exciting Information: In Collioure, take part in the traditional Catalan dance known as the Sardana. During special occasions, locals frequently congregate in the town square to perform this circle dance, asking everyone to join in and celebrate the culture of the area.

Chapter 6

Insider Tips for Different Types of Travelers

Are you going on a family trip? With the following family-friendly insider advice, you can make the most of your trip to Languedoc and Roussillon:

Parks with Adventures for All Ages

It is recommended that you spend a day of exhilarating enjoyment at Parc Aventure Fontdouce. This family-friendly adventure offers zip lines, treetop courses, and activities for all ages.

Beach Days in Collioure

Families will love the beaches in Collioure. Savour the mild waves of the Mediterranean while strolling around the lively alleys of the town. As a seashore snack, don't miss the renowned Collioure anchovies.

Enchanting Wineries For Families

Make a family-friendly winery visit, such as Domaine Gayda, where the kids can play in the dedicated play areas while you enjoy a guided tour. Parents and children both benefit from it.

Cité de l'Espace in Toulouse

Must-See Place: Spend a day trip to Toulouse and experience the instructive and amusing Cité de l'Espace, a space-themed park that is Ideal for families with future astronauts.

Solo Traveler's Guide

Languedoc and Roussillon provide a multitude of experiences suited for lone travellers, such as:

Hidden Gems in Pézenas

Insider Tip: The quaint alleyways and artisan stores of Pézenas are well-known. Explore off the beaten track to find undiscovered treasures, charming cafes, and stores that highlight the creative spirit of the town.

Solo Wine Tasting

Suggestion: Choose private wine tastings at upscale estates such as Château de Pennautier. Enjoy the wines and the tales that accompany them while conversing with winemakers.

Canal du Midi Cycling

Must-Do: Ride a solo bicycle tour along the gorgeous Canal du Midi. In Béziers, rent a bike and ride along the shady towpaths at your speed, discovering quaint communities.

Cathar Castles Solo Hike

Adventure Instructions: For a solitary excursion rich in history and expansive vistas, consider hiking to one of the Cathar Castles, such as Quéribus or Peyrepertuse. It's genuinely enchanted to be alone amidst historic ruin sites.

Advice For Senior Travelers

Are you a senior travelling? Use these senior-friendly suggestions to have a comfortable and easy time in Languedoc and Roussillon:

Beautiful Canal Boats

Advice: Take a leisurely trip down the Canal du Midi. Many trips have cosy boats so you can unwind and take in the gorgeous scenery.

Historic Train Journeys

Recommendation: It is recommended to discover the allure of the area by taking picturesque train journeys. The trip on the Train Jaune (Yellow Train) between Villefranche-de-Conflent and Latour-de-Carol is aesthetically pleasing and historically significant.

Relaxing Thermal Spas

[handwritten: 1hr 30min]

Must-See: Indulge in spa treatments in the area's hot springs, like Balaruc-les-Bains. Enjoy spa services that are intended to help you relax and rejuvenate while you unwind in the therapeutic waters.

Guided City Tours

Advice: When visiting cities such as Uzès or Carcassonne, choose guided tours. Numerous trips provide convenient transportation, making exploration educational and stress-free.

First-Timers' Checklist

If you're visiting Languedoc and Roussillon for the first time, make sure your introduction to the area is seamless and unforgettable by following this checklist:

Exploration of the Carcassonne Citadel

Must-See: Start with the recognisable Citadel of Carcassonne. Explore the Château Comtal, stroll through its mediaeval streets, and take in the spectacular views of the surrounding countryside.

Immersion in Local Markets

Important to consider: Get lost in the colourful neighbourhood markets, such as Uzès Market. Engage with amiable merchants while taking in the hues, tastes, and scents of local products.

Canal du Midi Boat Tour

Highlight: Take a cruise down the Canal du Midi, which is classified by UNESCO. Savour the serene beauty of this ancient canal whether you're on a boat or a stroll.

Don't miss the above, enjoy the experience in the Canal du Midi boat tour

Wine Tasting in Minervois

Not to be missed: Savour a wine tasting in Minervois. To taste the varied wines that define the area, visit well-known wineries like Château de Paraza.

With these insider recommendations, which are customised for various kinds of visitors, your trip through Languedoc and Roussillon is sure to be enjoyable and educational.

Domaine des Terres Georges, Minervois

Chapter 7

Accommodation and Dining

Options for Lodging

Discover a range of accommodation choices that suit various tastes and price ranges, guaranteeing a pleasant and unforgettable stay while you explore Languedoc and Roussillon:

Charming B&Bs in Saint-Guilhem-le-Désert

Highlight: Pick a bed and breakfast to fully experience Saint-Guilhem-le-Désert's charm. Anticipate friendly greetings, scenic surroundings, and tailored suggestions from your hosts. The usual price range for a night is between €80 and €120.

Luxurious Resorts in Collioure

Recommendation: Upgrade your Collioure vacation experience by choosing a posh resort on the Mediterranean coast. Savour opulent amenities, breathtaking views of the sea, and spa services. Luxurious resorts usually have nightly rates starting at €200.

Historic Carcassonne Hotels

Must-Try: Stay inside the ancient walls of one of Carcassonne's distinctive hotels to immerse yourself in its allure. These lodgings combine mediaeval charm with contemporary comforts. Historic hotels can cost between €120 and €250 a night.

Quaint Guesthouses in Pézenas

Insider Tip: Pézenas is home to charming guesthouses that embody the creative energy of the town. Savour a welcoming ambience and attentive service from your hosts. In general, guesthouses in Pézenas charge between €70 and €120 per night.

Eateries and Coffee Shops

Take a culinary tour of Languedoc and Roussillon with a carefully chosen assortment of eateries and cafes, each providing a unique eating experience:

Le Jardin de Saint-Adrien in Servian

Culinary Delight: Savour culinary treats at Le Jardin de Saint-Adrien, where inventive meals are made using ingredients that are acquired locally. A great dining experience should cost between €50 and €80 per person.

La Table de Fontfroide in Narbonne

Fine Dining: Located close to Narbonne in a former wine cellar, enjoy fine dining at La Table de Fontfroide. Enjoy sophisticated cuisine that emphasises local ingredients, with pricing per person ranging from €70 to €120 on average.

Nîmes's Les Halles Market

Tastes of the Locals: Take in the lively ambience of Nîmes' Les Halles Market. Visit one of the vibrant food vendors in the market to sample some local goods and have lunch. A market supper can cost anywhere between €15 and €30 per person.

Le Grand Cap in Leucate

Seaside Dining: Le Grand Cap in Leucate offers delicious seafood served right next to the ocean. Savour the fresh fish while taking in the expansive vistas, and budget between €40 and €60 per person for a filling dinner.

Specialties of Local Cuisine

Savour the distinct flavours of Languedoc and Roussillon with these regional delicacies, each of which offers a taste experience that pays homage to the rich culinary history of the area:

Cassoulet

The Best Place to Try: Castelnaudary's La Belle Époque is well-known for serving real cassoulet. Savour this filling dish that is made of a slow-cooked mixture of sausages, meats, and beans. A normal lunch of cassoulet costs between €20 and €30 per person.

Bouillabaisse

Signature Dish: When visiting Collioure, savour bouillabaisse, a typical fisherman's stew. Le Neptune is a restaurant that embodies this Provençal speciality and comes highly recommended. Although they can vary, bouillabaisse typically costs between €30 and €50 per person.

Brandade de Nîmes

Local Favourite: Savour the creamy combination of salt cod and olive oil, known as Brandade de Nîmes. For a local speciality with a Mediterranean twist, visit La Bodeguita in

Nîmes. Usually, Brandade de Nîmes costs between €15 and €25 per person.

Oysters from Bouzigues

Seafood Paradise: The fresh oysters of Bouzigues are highly recognised. Stop at l'Ecailler du Port for a delicious oyster buffet that highlights the flavours of the Thau Lagoon. Depending on the quantity, an oyster platter might cost anywhere from €15 to €30.

Oysters from Bouzigues

Chapter 8

Transportation and Getting Around

Travelling to Roussillon and Languedoc

Setting out for Languedoc and Roussillon is an exhilarating start to the voyage ahead. To go to this charming area, think about the following options:

Air Travel

Airports closest to the region: Montpellier-Méditerranée Airport (MPL), Perpignan-Rivesaltes Airport (PGF), and Carcassonne Airport (CCF) are the main airports servicing Languedoc and Roussillon. Depending on the time of year and season, round-trip airfare from major European cities to these airports can cost anything from €100 to €400 or more.

Train Travel

High-Speed Rail (TGV): The TGV, France's high-speed rail system, offers productive connections. Train terminals in major cities such as Montpellier and Nîmes are well connected. For instance, the cost of a one-way TGV ticket from Paris to Montpellier might range from €50 to €100, based on the class and time of booking.

Car Travel

Deciding to go on a picturesque drive? Major highways provide accessibility to the area. Depending on the type of vehicle and rental company, a week's worth of automobile rental can run you anywhere from €200 to €400.

Local Transportation in the Regions

Discovering the undiscovered beauties and cultural treasures of Languedoc and Roussillon requires travelling through their varied landscapes. Select from the following modes of transportation:

Local Buses and Trains

Effective Connectivity: Towns and cities are connected by a vast network of regional trains and buses. Regional rail tickets can cost anything from €10 to €30, depending on the distance travelled, for example, from Montpellier to Nîmes.

Rental Cars

Travel Flexibility: Hiring a car gives you more freedom, particularly when visiting places that are less frequented. The daily rental rate might vary based on the type of car and length of the rental, typically ranging from €30 to €80.

Cycling

Routes de Scène: Take a bicycle tour through the breathtaking scenery of Languedoc and Roussillon. Bike rentals are available in several places, with daily rates ranging from €15 to €30.

Boat Tours

Canal du Midi: Take a boat tour to see the stunning Canal du Midi. A one-day cruise can cost anywhere between €30 to €70, depending on the itinerary and extras offered.

Car Rental Tips

For a seamless and pleasurable travel experience, bear the following advice in mind if you decide to rent a car for its flexibility:

Advance Booking

Cost savings: Reserve your rental car in advance to get the best deals. This can save you as much as 20% or more and guarantees availability.

Verify Your Insurance Coverage

Comprehensive Coverage: Examine the insurance that the rental company provides. For peace of mind, think about getting extra coverage. You should budget an additional €10 to €20 each day for insurance.

GPS or App for Navigation:

Navigational Assistance: Use a smartphone navigation app or make sure your rental car has GPS. This is very useful for scenic route navigation. The price range for renting a GPS is €5 to €10 per day.

Fuel Rules

Understanding Terms: Become acquainted with the rental company's fuel policy. Some may have distinct policies, such as requiring you to return the vehicle with the tank full.

Parking Requirements

Accommodations: If you are staying in a tiny village or the heart of a city, make sure your lodging has parking available. While some locations could have parking available on-site, others might have possibilities close by.

Chapter 9

Safety and Health

Safety Considerations

It is crucial to make sure you are secured when touring Languedoc and Roussillon. To ensure a safe and pleasurable trip, heed these safety pieces of advice:

Cultural Knowledge

Tips: Honour regional traditions and customs. Gaining an understanding of the cultural quirks improves the experience and encourages constructive communication.

Pickpocket Vigilance: Exercise caution when in busy areas, at tourist sites, and on public transit. Make use of money belts and other anti-theft devices, and safeguard your valuables.

Travel Insurance

You are advised to give travel insurance priority. It offers protection against unforeseen events, medical emergencies, and trip cancellations. Make sure your policy meets your unique requirements.

Being Weather Prepared

A piece of advice: Consider the local weather when packing. Especially in the summer, always have plenty of drink, a hat, and sunscreen with you.

Respect for Nature

Advice: Respect wildlife and stick to authorised pathways when exploring natural regions. Keep an eye out for wildlife in the area, carry a map, and use caution when in uncharted territory.

Emergency Phone Numbers

It's important to know who to contact in an emergency. To ensure a safe stay, keep these emergency numbers handy:

- Police Emergency Number: 17
- Emergency Medical/Ambulance Services: 15
- Department of Fire: 18
- European Emergency Number: 112

For specific tourist police contacts, inquire at the local tourism bureaus.

Medical and Health Facilities

Place your health and the availability of medical facilities in the area first.

Clinics and Hospitals

★ **Montpellier University Medical Centre**

Address: 191 Avenue du Doyen Gaston Giraud, 34295 Montpellier

GPS Coordinates: 43.6321° N, 3.8533° E

Telephone: +33 4 67 33 67 33

★ **Perpignan Hospital**

Address: 20 Avenue du Languedoc, 66000 Perpignan

GPS Coordinates: 42.6931° N, 2.8863° E

Telephone: +33 4 68 61 66 33

Pharmacy Stores

Pharmacy closest to Montpellier

Address: 1 Place Paul Bec, 34000 Montpellier

GPS Coordinates: 43.6135° N, 3.8782° E

Telephone: +33 4 67 92 18 58

The pharmacy closest to you in Perpignan

Address: 27 Avenue de Grande-Bretagne, 66000 Perpignan

GPS Coordinates: 42.6985° N, 2.8832° E

Telephone: +33 4 68 35 07 02

Travellers' Medical Services

★ **Montpellier's International SOS Clinic**

Address: 287 Rue Helene Boucher, 34170 Castelnau-le-Lez

GPS Coordinates: 43.6402° N, 3.9142° E

Telephone: +33 4 67 07 70 70

Measures For Protecting Your Health

Immunisations: For specific recommendations and immunisations, speak with your healthcare professional.

First Aid Kit for Travel

Essentials: Bring bandages, basic drugs, and any prescription medications you may need in your travel first aid kit.

Recall that putting your health and safety first guarantees a worry-free trip in Languedoc and Roussillon. Become familiar with the emergency services in your area and keep important contacts close to hand.

Chapter 10

Language and Communication

Basics of Language

Although Languedoc and Roussillon are officially bilingual, here are some linguistic skills to improve your communication:

Greetings:

- Hello: Bonjour (bohn-zhoor)
- Goodbye: Au revoir (oh reh-vwar)
- Please: S'il vous plaît (seel voo pleh)
- Thank you: Merci (mehr-see)

Customary Etiquette

- Excuse me / I'm sorry: Excusez-moi (ehk-skew-zay mwah)

- Yes: Oui (wee)
- No: Non (noh)
- Pardon / What?: Pardon / Quoi ? (pahr-dohn / kwa)

Numbers

1: Un (uh)

2: Deux (duh)

3: Trois (twah)

4: Quatre (katr)

5: Cinq (sank)

Handy Expressions

Improve your conversations by using these helpful terms:

- I need help, please: J'ai besoin d'aide, s'il vous plaît (zhay buh-ZWAH duh-eed, seel voo pleh).

- Where is...?: Où est... ? (oo eh)
- ...the train station?: ...la gare ? (la gar)
- ...the bathroom?: ...les toilettes ? (lay twa-let)
- ...a pharmacy?: ...une pharmacie ? (ewn far-ma-see)
- I would like...: Je voudrais... (zhuh voo-dray)
- ...a coffee: ...un café (uhn kah-fay)
- ...the check, please: ...l'addition, s'il vous plaît (la-dee-syon, seel voo pleh)
- Help!: À l'aide ! (ah layd)
- I don't understand: Je ne comprends pas (zhuh nuh kohm-prahn pah)

Tips On Communication

It can be satisfying to navigate foreign language conversation. Examine these suggestions:

1. **Learn important words**: Acquire the fundamental phrases to be courteous and request help. The people here value your efforts.
2. **Use apps for translation:** Download translation applications to get help quickly. They can support you in both spoken and written language.
3. **Talk clearly and slowly:** Speak clearly and slowly when in French. This makes understanding easier, particularly for non-native English speakers.
4. **Discover local accents:** People may speak different dialects in remote places. For a more fulfilling experience, become acquainted with some popular phrases in these dialects.
5. **Accept nonverbal correspondence:** Be mindful of nonverbal clues. Body language, facial expressions, and gestures are frequently used to convey meaning in French culture.

6. **Take part in language exchange:** Have a language conversation with the locals. They might help you get better in French in return for your interest in their language.

Don't be a loner, communicate with locals!

Chapter 11

Practical Information

Currency and Banking

- Money: The Euro (€) is the official currency.
- Finance: On weekdays, banking hours are normally from 9 AM to 5 PM.
- ATMs are generally accessible for easy cash withdrawals in towns and cities.
- Although most places accept credit cards, it's a good idea to have extra cash on hand for smaller businesses.

Plug Types and Electricity

- Electricity: 50 Hz is the frequency, and 230 V is the standard voltage. Commonly used outlets include Type C and Type E.

- Plug types: European two-pin Type C, French two-pin type E
- It is advised that you pack an appropriate adaptor for your electronic equipment.

Connectivity And The Internet

- *Internet:* In public areas, coffee shops, and hotels, Wi-Fi is generally available.
- If you want dependable mobile internet coverage, get a local SIM card.
- *Connectivity:* Although Roussillon and Languedoc have decent mobile network coverage, signal strength may be weak in some rural locations.

Local Rules and Statutes

- Legal Drinking Age: Eighteen is the legal drinking age.

- Smoking Policies: It is not permitted to smoke in enclosed public areas. Recognise where smoking is allowed.

Cultural Awareness

- When you visit places of worship, wear modest clothing.
- Steer clear of boisterous discussions in public areas.

Traffic Rules

- Drive on the right side of the road.
- Seat belts are mandatory for all occupants.

Security Services: The police, ambulance, and fire department's emergency number is 112.

Chapter 12

Itineraries and Day Trips

One-Week Itinerary for Roussillon and Languedoc

Day 1-2: Montpellier

- Discover Montpellier Cathedral, Place de la Comédie, and the old centre.
- For those interested in art, visit Musée Fabre.
- Take a stroll around Ecusson and Antigone, two lively neighbourhoods.

Day 3-4: Carcassonne

- Explore the Carcassonne mediaeval fortification.
- Explore the Basilica of Saint-Nazaire and take a stroll around the city walls.

- Savour regional food in the quaint Old Town.

Day 5–6: Perpignan and Collioure

- Unwind at Collioure, a charming seaside village.
- Enjoy the beaches and a visit to the Royal Castle.
- Discover Perpignan, a bustling city with strong Catalan influences.

Day 7: Nîmes

- See the remains of the Roman Empire, such as the Maison Carrée and the Arena of Nîmes.
- Explore the Diana Temple and the Jardins de la Fontaine.

Two-Week Exploration Itinerary

Week 1: Languedoc Highlights

- Stick to the previous one-week schedule.

- Explore the mediaeval charm of Saint-Guilhem-le-Désert.
- Take a look at the Roman aqueduct Pont du Gard and unwind by the Gardon River.

Week 2: Extended Discoveries and Roussillon

- Proceed to the seaside village of Collioure.
- Learn about the fascinating fusion of cultures in the dynamic city of Perpignan.
- Travel to the Côte Vermeille to see breathtaking views of the seashore.

Recommended Day Trips

Day Trip 1: Pont du Gard and Uzès

- See the famous Pont du Gard, which is included as a UNESCO World Heritage Site.

- Explore Uzès, a mediaeval town with a picturesque market square.

Day Trip 2: Minerve and Saint-Chinian

- Explore Minerve, a mediaeval village renowned for its natural bridges.
- Discover the Saint-China region's vineyards and sample its wines.

Day Trip 3: Narbonne and the Abbaye de Fontfroide

- Explore the peaceful Cistercian monastery, Abbaye de Fontfroide.
- Discover the Archbishop's Palace and the Canal de la Robine as you stroll through the old city of Narbonne.

These travel plans offer a unique combination of cultural immersion, historical exploration, and scenic splendour.

Tailor to individual interests and preferences to guarantee an unforgettable trip in Languedoc and Roussillon.

A tower in Roussillon

Languedoc and Roussillon Travel Guide 2024

Conclusion

Imagine yourself setting off on a journey through Languedoc and Roussillon, weaving together historical marvels, cultural riches, and the stunning scenery of southern France, like a tapestry. Discover the captivating stories hidden in every part of this region, ranging from the mediaeval grandeur of Carcassonne to the coastal attractiveness of Collioure.

Take in the colourful marketplaces, relish the mouthwatering regional cuisine, and allow the ghosts of antiquity to lead you about. Languedoc and Roussillon emerge as a mosaic of experiences, offering something for every traveller, whether they are history buffs, wine connoisseurs, or nature lovers.

Share Your Feedback

It is our aim that this travel guide will be a useful tool for you, enhancing your trip and revealing the lesser-known attractions in Languedoc and Roussillon. Your input is very important to us, and we would be happy to hear about your experiences and any ideas you may have to improve our guide.

Please feel free to offer any advice, ideas, or other details you think would be helpful to other travellers. Your input helps us to keep our travel resources getting better.

Bon Voyage!

Printed in Great Britain
by Amazon